Royal Navy Basic Training

Royal Navy Basic Training

The diary of a new recruit

C. MOTH

Published by CMoth Publishing

A CIP catalogue record for this book is available from the British Library.

ISBN 978-1-7398470-0-5

Contents

Preface

My daughter joined the Royal Navy at the age of 17. She was fresh out of school but did not want to carry on with formal education as she believed this future was not for her. So often we try to fit a 'square peg into a round hole', as we think it's the best for our children, but in this case it was obvious early on that practical qualifications were the way to go. As I come from a family who have Navy in their blood, I suggested the Royal Navy, knowing they had an exceptional training programme and career structure. I made it quite clear that my daughter could not leave college, unless she was going into a structured programme. After completing the rigorous Naval selection process from interviews, fitness tests and numeracy and reasoning tests, she finally made it to HMS Raleigh.

It has been two years now since I dropped my daughter off at Plymouth Train Station, and neither she (nor I) have any regrets at all. Yes, there have been plenty of 'ups and downs' but it was the right decision. I was so proud watching her 'passing out' at HMS Raleigh. I cannot thank the Raleigh instructors enough – without their dedication and support Raleigh would not be such a great training facility. In ten weeks, they take hundreds of young men and women from a world of social media, and in some cases 'mollycoddled' individuals, and make them into sailors ready to move on to their Phase 2 training. Much of what the recruits learn at Raleigh are the basic skills that are missing from much of our education system. I am a firm believer that in education it's not all about exam results – there is so much more to learn in life.

The following diary is based on my daughter's experience of the Royal Navy Basic Training at HMS Raleigh. It has been written to help recruits before they join HMS Raleigh, so they have some idea what to expect. HMS Raleigh is the Royal Navy's Initial Training School located at Torpoint, Cornwall. All names have been changed for confidentiality.

Navy words used at Raleigh

IMF	Initial Military Fitness
Mess deck	the floor
PVR	Pre-voluntary Release
Heads	toilets
Cleaning ship/ Clearing the decks	cleaning accommodation
No. 4	blue rig
No. 3	black trousers, white shirt, blue jumper, blue 'woolly poolly'
No. 2	officer uniform
No. 1	sailor's uniform, posh uniform
Bish'	Chaplain
Scran	food
Call to Hands	wake up
DOs	Divisional Officers
PTIs	Physical Training Instructors
Pipe down	go to bed
DUDT	Discharged Unsuitable During Training

NAAFI	Navy, Army and Air Force Institutes (NAAFI) but it's just the shop
PRNC	Pre-Royal Navy Course
AFCO	Armed Forces Career Office
NSRT	Naval Service Recruitment Test
PJFT	Pre-joining Fitness Test

Pre-Raleigh

The Christmas before I officially joined the Navy, my mum took me to the Portsmouth careers office (Armed Forces Career Office – AFCO) to talk about a career in the Royal Navy. I started college but wasn't really enjoying studying anymore and wanted to do something practical. Luckily, my mum understood that A-levels are not for everyone, but she would only let me look at other career options if they were structured and would ultimately lead to further vocational qualifications. When children go to school it becomes a conveyor belt of expectations, you have to do well in your SATs, followed by GCSEs, followed by A-levels, followed by a degree. This route, although promoted by schools, is not the only route and isn't right for everyone. I remember telling my mum in the first autumn half term at college that I really wasn't enjoying studying, and regretted not pursuing a practical qualification. The next thing I knew I was sitting in a room, at the Royal Navy careers office, with a female Petty Officer who was in the Royal Navy surface fleet.

The Petty Officer was very enthusiastic and loved the Navy, you could tell. She joined when she was 20 years old and never regretted it. She loved HMS Raleigh, although I now suspect it's one of those things you can look back on with 'rose tinted glasses', and you forget about the bad bits! She said she made friends for life at

Raleigh but all her fellow recruits went on to different branches. She was right, after HMS Raleigh all my fellow recruits dispersed to different training bases around the country and then later on different ships, countries, and seas around the world. Some of the recruits I trained with are now on HMS *Queen Elizabeth*, our flagship aircraft carrier, whereas some of them are on smaller destroyers, patrolling the English Channel, and some are 100 metres below in a V class submarine.

After my talk with the Chief Petty Officer, I attended a presentation on the Royal Navy and different branches. The discussion was on the different branches and the application process. It sounded very straightforward, but picking a branch was difficult and, in fact, I changed my branch a few times during the application process. Unfortunately, there didn't seem that much information on the different roles, apart from what was obvious, Chefs go into Catering, Writers go into Logistics etc., but perhaps the Navy cannot really say what the submarine service does and it's a bit hard to imagine it as well. I didn't really decide on my chosen role and branch until I went to the PRNC (Pre-Royal Navy Course) and a female officer gave a talk on the submarine service.

After the initial carers talk at Christmas, I completed my application form and submitted it. At this point, I wasn't sure about joining but it was only an application form. After Christmas, I was called in to complete the Naval Service Recruitment Test (NSRT), which is a written test recruits complete on general reasoning, verbal ability, numeracy and mechanical comprehension. I was quite nervous but found it ok; some of it was like sitting a

GCSE maths paper. I had 45 minutes to complete the test and the result of it would decide which role you were/weren't qualified for. For example, mine clearance divers and a navy nurse might need a higher score than chefs. There was about ten of us sitting the test, everyone looked nervous, after the test we were told to sit in the reception. Myself and three other teenagers were called in together and told we had passed. Relief!

I was never told my exact score after the test, just told I could apply for most roles. Apparently, they don't publish the requirements for the roles and the NSRT results, but I had a backup role, if it was needed.

After the NSRT, I waited for my interview date, which was another month. I changed my AFCO to my local one and went along, dressed smartly. The PO at the branch called me into his office and asked me some general questions about the Royal Navy: Why I wanted to join? Why I did I want to be in logistics (my original choice)? At the end of the interview, I was told to wait in the reception and was then called back in. The PO said I had passed the interview, and was given handouts on fitness training and what to expect next.

Then there was about a two-month wait for my medical and eyesight test. You have a pre-medical consultation on the phone before the physical test called 'the triage'. My dad drove me up to Crawley, and I waited outside the doctor's office before I was called in. You had to wait a few days for the results of the medical. I was very relieved when I was passed, as you hear about people going to the medical and the doctor finding conditions that recruits never knew they had. If they find a walking gait or shin splints and then that's it, it can all be over. There are some medical conditions that mean you just cannot join. I had read about the medical beforehand and read that some recruits fail the medical first time, so it was nerve-racking. Before completing the physical medical, I had to complete a medical questionnaire that is discussed by the medical practitioner. At the physical the doctor weighed me, measured my height and I did some exercises: eye and hearing test, breathing exercises, funny walks. Oh, and I also had to do some press-ups in my underwear... a bit weird really.

It's funny how the more you progress through the joining process the more you want to join. It feels like there's one hurdle after the next before you're allowed in. Once my medical test was done, I was declared fit to progress, and next it was the wait for the fitness test. To be honest the wait was quite quick, and around April I went to the Nuffield Health Centre for my PJFT. The Pre-joining Fitness Test (PJFT) involved completing a 2.4 km run on a treadmill. I went up to Gatwick to the Nuffield Centre and waited for the fitness instructor to start the test. The centre was really nice and not your standard gym. There were at least 20 treadmills. I had only run outside, so I was a bit worried about running on a treadmill, but I need not have been, as if anything it was easier. I was shown how to work the running machine, a good thing! The instructor did a full warm up with me before the test started. The advantage to the treadmill is you can see all the statistics on how long you have left etc., but you really just have to go for it. My target time for my age and height was 13 minutes and 10 seconds, and I managed it in 11 minutes and 59 seconds, so I was pleased it was a pass with a bit of time to spare. I was quite chuffed when I came out and gave my mum a big sweaty hug. Another hurdle done and next onto the PRNC.

My Pre-Royal Navy Course (PRNC) was in June and was a four-day course at HMS Collingwood, Fareham. This was a four-day introduction to life in the Royal Navy, and you either passed or failed it. I'm not sure if you still have to do this, as there was talk of this going, but I had to go. The course is a mini-introduction to basic training. I arrived at Fareham train station in smart clothes and could easily spot the other recruits. We were met by the Navy staff and boarded the minibus for Collingwood. Once we got to Collingwood, I was given my ID card, kit and water bottle; all of which had to be labelled. We then went to a seminar room and were given introductions to the PRNC and what we were to expect. There were quite a few presentations over the next few days, covering topics like the ethos of the Royal Navy, behaviour, and introductions to the different branches, and this when I decided to change my branch to the submarine service. A female officer gave a talk on the submarine service and that was it, I was hooked. I never thought in a million years I would want to be in a submarine, but I did and the rest is history, as they say. It also helped that you are paid more in the submarine service! After the briefs we went out to the parade ground for an introduction to drill, nothing too strenuous, a lot of 'shuffling' going on, but all in all not a bad effort for a bunch of newbies. Most of the day we spent on drill and then were taught how to make beds and hospital corners.

The next day we had the swimming test. The test is the same as the one at HMS Raleigh which consists of swimming 50 metres in a boiler suit then hoisting yourself out the water. You have to tread water for two minutes before the swim followed by swimming circuits, which were pass/ fail so it's just about showing you are giving your all at 100% at all times. The day ended with bullying our boots.

Friday started with 'scran' and followed by the fitness run. It wasn't that long ago I did the fitness test, so I felt like I should be ok. The difference, however, is when you do the fitness test for the selection process, you just show up, warm up and do your timed run, but in PRNC, and at Raleigh, it's not like that. You are woken up at 5.30 am, marched for hours, then perhaps you'll do some circuits, and then you'll do the fitness test, so make sure you're fitter than the minimum as you need to be! We all passed and my time was around 11 minutes, so faster than the required time. The afternoon was great, as we did our ship's visit to HMS *Diamond* in Portsmouth Harbour. HMS *Diamond* is a one of our newer Type 45 destroyers, and looks like the *Starship Enterprise* inside; it is quite incredible to see in person. Once the four days were over, we were taken back to Fareham train station. I enjoyed the PRNC and did see some of the same recruits again, when I joined in September, so you can end up with the same people at Raleigh. It was around now joining the Royal Navy started to feel like a reality.

Week 1

Arriving at HMS Raleigh

Sunday 1st September

13.00 – Here I am at Plymouth train station with one suitcase and the clothes I'm wearing. Smart clothes, of course, but I am furnishing a rather dodgy haircut. I've got my hair up, but it is died black, and I have the sides shaved. My mum left; she didn't come into the station with me, as I'm not good at goodbyes. A quick hug and a wave and she was on her way back to Brighton. I felt like running. I always thought I'd get here and then run off. I think that's probably why my mum brought me so I didn't run off, but I don't want to disappoint her.

There are a few other new recruits here. It's obvious as we are all dressed smartly and the boys have shaved heads; a dead giveaway. Everyone looks like deer in headlights, and I suspect they are all as scared as I am feeling. Everyone is quiet though. A few recruits chat to each other with the usual questions: where did you come from? etc... but it's a fairly brisk conversation. We are not here long before the Navy guys turn up, looking cheerful, probably thinking fresh meat to the grinder! They introduce themselves and start ticking off our names. Could I run off now? I'm was certainly thinking about, but it's too late before I know it we're all chaperoned onto the bus like sheep... no escape.

We arrive at Raleigh, after a 30-minute trip across the water on the Torpoint ferry that crosses over to where the Navy base is. Plymouth is actually a nice city when looking back from the water, but we are soon driving pass some dodgy looking houses towards the base. HMS Raleigh looks like a prison from the outside. The base has high fences with barbed wire running around it, and the staff on the gate are holding rifles and have that look of 'Don't mess with me, mate'. The buildings vary from pleasantly designed white brick ones to some semi high rises of 1970s build; the base is huge. It has a parade ground that's a couple of hundred square metres and some huge plane hangars where indoor 'passing outs' occur if the weather is 'naff'. The view is quite stunning across the river to the far-off Cornish hills but there is no time for looking. We are all marched off the buses to a seminar room. It's comical really, as no one has really marched before, except a few keen ex-cadets, so it looks we look like a 'bunch of Muppets'.

At the introduction we were told about the ghosts in Raleigh; during a bombing at the start of WW2, 65 Navy personnel were killed and apparently they still haunt the parade ground at night, a good reason not to go on it at night. Also, you're not allowed to whistle in the Royal Navy, because in the 18th century whistling was used to communicate the start of the Nore Mutiny, but apparently if you're a chef you can whistle as it means you're not eating the 'scran' or spitting in it! Anyway, so whistling is out.

At the end of my bunk is a box with our uniform in it that we have to try on. We are issued with our kit, Number 3,

Number 4s, socks, shirts and boots. They say you could literally turn up here with nothing and the Navy would look after you, and that actually is true. All the new recruits are shown how to place our kit in the lockers and then we all go down to the seminar room for a briefing from the chief. We have to give in any 'extras' we have brought with us, so extra sweets, chocolate all have to be binned. I put all the chocolate in my stored bag in the hope I can access it later.

OMG – I have to share a room (mess deck) with 30 other strangers... The mess deck is literally the size of a classroom with 30 recruits squeezed into it: each with a small bed and a small locker. Ok, I know it could be worse, at least I'm not camping. Although this is not a ship everything is named as if it were on one. It is like 'let's pretend' on a grand scale. We all wear the same clothes and are treated the same, no matter on your background. There are a lot of 'Northerners' here and accents from all over the world. Some, like the Scottish accents, can be a bit hard to understand, but I imagine I'll get used to it. I'm tired after a long day of travel and chatting to other recruits. 22.30 seems like an early time for lights out, but I think I'll sleep.

Monday 2nd September

05.30 – it is 5 o'clock in the morning and generally I only get up at this 'kind of' hour if I have to get on a plane. We are marched for 'scran' (which means food) and all look at each other nervously in silence. I think some of the boys may be at breakfast in body only and their brains have yet to wake up, but I feel the same.

This is now officially paperwork day. I have completed so much paperwork and signed so many papers that my eyes are burning. I've done more paperwork today than I did for my entire GCSEs, which is probably why I'm here. I now have a will... my mum and sister can have all my worldly goods... not much really: my phone, some Nike Air Forces, probably not enough to retire on.

I am now pretty much owned by the Royal Navy for the next four weeks after which time I can request to leave... so my first escape is in four weeks' time... mmm. It's called PVR (Pre-voluntary Release), but you can't do it for four weeks. For at least four weeks the Navy own me and 'hard luck'. I'm not going anywhere. I am officially in the Nelson Division, in Port Class. There are six divisions at Raleigh: Hanson, Nelson, Cornwell, Gould, Fisher and Cunningham, with Ganges (holdover divisions) and Crean (sick bay). I quite like being in the Nelson Division, as my mum was originally from Portsmouth and dragged me and my sister around the Historic Dockyards and HMS *Victory* on many a summer's day. HMS *Victory* was where we always took relatives that came to visit us so it's comforting being in a division with a familiar name.

Amidst all the paperwork and seminars today we managed to fit in the fitness run. I quite like the fitness part, or did; we have to run 2.4 km as fast as we can. We were told that we had to beat the appropriate time for our age. In ten weeks' time I have to improve on the time I managed today, so you want to go fast but not too fast... that's what I thought! Once you're out on the astro courts, with the PT instructors screaming at you, you tend to go as fast as you can. This morning for breakfast you could have a full English breakfast, I'm not a huge fan and went for porridge and now I'm glad. Some of the lads in my division threw up most of their breakfast on the way round, but, impressively, still managed to make the cut-off time. I thought swearing at recruits was only in the movies, but the language was very colourful. A couple of recruits failed their run and are moved to Crean to improve their fitness; a move referred to as 'going to fat camp' at Raleigh. It's almost like they passed their fitness run in the interview and then did no preparation before joining Raleigh. 'Fat camp' is where these recruits will spend a few weeks getting their fitness up to a level where they can resume their training.

Shower time! Bloody 'ell it's group showers! My mum said when she was at school they had group showers after PE lessons in the 1980s; I thought she was having me on but the Navy still has them in training. I have never showered with other women – until now. I thought this was illegal… my shower was quick. Funny the older women didn't care. They strutted into the showers as if they owned the place. Us 'youngsters' were a bit shyer about it all, ran in, and out pretty quickly. You don't really have much time to think about the group showering, as you're in such a hurry to get in and out, and onto the next activity. All I can say is, I hope we only have group showers in Basic Training.

Wednesday 4th September

I spent most of the morning kit marking. If your kit is not named properly you fail your kit muster. I also had to sew my name onto some bits of my uniform, including my PT wear. The kit muster is when you lay out all your kit, named, washed and ironed ready for the inspection. All shirts have to be folded at the correct measurement and in the correct format; this is called 'ship's book size' and is an A4 size. There is a picture of the correct layout in our mess deck for us to check against. There are four golden rules that will fail your kit muster. These are: Wet, Dirty, Missing and Unmarked. I would like to say I practiced ironing and folding before I came to Raleigh, but I didn't, so it was a steep learning curve. You spend hours naming your kit. I took a couple of white laundry markers with and got through them in no time at all.

Over the course of the Navy training, we had Initial Military Fitness (IMF) sessions. Some sadistic PT instructor beasts you for an hour. As we march into the gym hall the PT instructors start screaming at us to 'hurry up and get onto your spots'. There are spots on the floor that we have to stand on, spaced apart. The PT instructor came over to one of the lads, Recruit Marshall, and ripped off his name tag that he had just sewn on, saying that it wasn't sewn on straight and he now needs to resew it for the next IMF.

I haven't climbed a rope since primary school, and even then I found it hard but now, crikey, I managed about two metres, which was more than some recruits. Some of the fit guys sped to the top of the ropes. One lad got to the top and the PT instructors told him to wait there before the rest of the recruits were off the ground. It was a rule that you had to face forward, but I could see his grip slipping through the corner of my eye. In about a split second he had fallen 30 foot onto his knees. The instructors carried on screaming at him and wouldn't let him leave the session despite all the limping. (It wasn't till the next morning, when his knee had swollen to the size of a small football, they let him go to sickbay just to find that he had torn his ACL and would be in rehab for the next ten months.) The only good bit about the IMFs are the instructors are 'buff' and that's about it. Sit ups, press ups, burpees running on the spot, you name it, we did it at double time.

We end the day 'cleaning ship' before bed duty. In other words cleaning the mess deck and checking everyone is in bed before lights out at 22.30. Slept like a log.

Friday 6th September

Early start again today getting my kit ready and 'cleaning the decks'. This was followed by the pool. I really enjoy swimming, so I actually freakishly looked forward to the swim test. A fifty metre swim followed by two minutes treading water in our number 4s…that's the blue boiler suits, which become very heavy when wet; it's not the same as treading water with a swim suit on. Think about putting on a mechanics canvas overall and trying to swim in it. The hardest part was trying to get out of an old Victorian swim pool with high sides with a wet boiler suit on, it was tough and not surprisingly you can't use the steps. There is a distance of half a metre between the water and the side, so you 'haul' yourself up like a beached whale, flapping and grunting.

The swim was followed by jumping off the high board, which is about three metres off the ground. It was called the high board, unless you're really scared of heights, and when you get to the top and look down it feels really high! It is supposed to simulate jumping off the side of the ship, so you jump with your hands either side. I really didn't enjoy jumping off; you walk to the edge of the board and just step off without stopping, which makes it extra scary. Recruit Taylor, a fellow female recruit, just refused to jump. She got to the edge of the board looked down and just froze. Taylor had to be helped down the stairs because she was shaking so much. We all tried to encourage her but it was no use but she'll will get another attempt. I think the trick is not to look down, just get to the edge of the board, cross your arms and go for it. All your fellow recruits are shouting and encouraging you so it feels like a team effort. If you fail though, you get another chance, so it's not all over, unfortunately Taylor just couldn't jump even after numerous attempts, and encouragement, so was discharged after a few weeks.

After the swim we were marched back to our block and wait outside to be dismissed. In the distance there's people shouting and group of pale faces trooped ran past us. They stop, and the girls lagging behind are screamed at. "Don't roll your frecking eyes at me" screams the instructor. One of the girls stops and wobbles, then she pukes... I was in shock. Too late now though, I'm here for the next four weeks of my life, I think to myself.

Saturday 7th September

05.30 – I woke up today knowing I had a whole day of ironing and washing in front of me. Just think a couple of weeks ago I had a mum to do my laundry for me; I have to spend hours in the wash and iron room doing it all by hand. My hands are actually raw and very cracked from all the hand washing. Vaseline would help if I had some.

We had flight deck sports this morning, which was brilliant fun. We were split into two teams by our divisional staff and competed against each other by holding some of our teammates up on PE mats. Whilst being held up in the air, we had to run across the sports hall, it was hysterical and loads of fun. It was a great bonding experience for our class and a great laugh. It was so nice to be able to laugh out loud and not worry that someone was going to tell you off. We also did pudding races where one person jumps on a PE mat to make it slide as far as possible across the hall and then you rotate between members of your team. I haven't laughed so much in ages.

Sunday 8th September

Sunday is the best day of the week. I know I'll say this a few times but it definitely is a great day. We have a lie in until 7 am. At church, we sing hymns and enjoy not being screamed at. Church is bit like being at 'home' and brings us down to earth. We are also allowed our mobile phones and have tea and biscuits after; little things really matter now. For the first four weeks of training, you're not allowed a cup of tea or NAFFI privileges, outside of 'scran', which you miss a lot. If you're used to Costa or Starbucks, then forget it. The only time you get a tea is at breakfast. As the weeks go by you have to earn privileges, and when finally you'll able to get a hot drink it makes such a difference to your morale.

Week 1 Statistics:

PVRs in the class – 0

IMF completed – 2

Week 2

IMFs

Monday 9th September

05.30 – We start with 'call to hands' being piped three times, which means getting up at some horrendous hour followed by a quick group shower and tidy up before inspection. The divisional staff come round, inspect the decks and kit, with the Warrant Officer. The Chief seem to throw 'things' around just for the fun of it but it's intense, and they are very 'picky'. If you don't pass the kit inspection you are dismissed, so it's not a game, although somewhat feels like one. I spent hours this weekend preparing my kit so that it was all laid out neatly on my bed, but we all still got a pretty good telling off for the state of the mess deck. My bedroom was never this tidy!

The Divisional Officers (DOs) seem to just walk in our mess decks and just start throwing kit off the bed. We spend ages ironing, washing, folding and then in about ten minutes it's all thrown around. One of the recruits left a cereal box in the lockers, and the DOs found it and then just emptied the contents all over the floor. After we had tidied up the mess, made by the kit inspectors, we were marched over to the parade ground for drill. It's so funny. The drill instructor is a short Marine, who doesn't hold back, and when he screams the veins on his neck stick out. Again, all I can say is I'm glad I'm not a redhead! Left, right, left right, two words that seem easy but 30 recruits marching in time is not so easy. We practiced left and right turns, whilst trying to stay in line. The words 'into line, left turn' and 'into line, right turn' were shouted at us and practised again and again, with no let-up. Sometimes our class got it spot on and other times it was a complete shambles, this was all followed by more popping out veins and screaming by the marine drill instructor. There's always one recruit who just doesn't get it and Recruit McDonald just could not get his left and rights sorted in his head, which made the whole drill practice more difficult.

Drill gets quite tiring as you're on your feet the whole time but at least it doesn't take much thought. Even though I'm tired, we march back to the decks to get changed for IMF number 3. It is relentless it never feels like you get a break to do anything; you're not even allowed to sit down and rest. I actually took myself off to the toilet today for five minutes, so I could sit down without being told off. I sat in the 'heads' listening to a girl next door sobbing into her hands, I know how she feels; it is just 'knackering'. The toilets become the escape room to let it all out in the next few weeks. It's not just the girls, I've seen the lads crying in the ironing room as well... it's tough for everyone. Each individual activity is not difficult or tiring, but when you put them all back to back, without a break, it is. At home, school, even work you get a rest break but not at Basic Training, it's nonstop with no let up, ever.

Today the class leaders were chosen... haha... some recruits really want to be class leaders but at the end of the day it's more work, and you are responsible for your division's 'screw ups'; I fear there may be many! If anyone is late to any activity, the class leader is responsible and there are some recruits who just seem to do everything wrong, late etc. Recruit McDonald just seems to get into trouble and comes across as a bit 'dippy'. Of course you don't have phones with you during the day, so you need to rely on a clock and most of us bought cheap watches, which are invaluable, In the Navy you have to make sure you're five minutes early for everything, and it's no different at Raleigh, if you're late, you're punished and so is your class.

22.30 – pipe down.

Tuesday 10th September

In Nelson's mess deck there are four bunks in each row and to the left of my bunk is Recruit Munro. She is from St Lucia, and has two children back at home. She misses them greatly and has that 'mummy feel' to her. She's great because she's in her 30s, and seems older and wiser than us teenagers, so we can go to her with our problems. She's good at putting it all into perspective, although I fear she's also going through a lot. My mum sends me 'care packages' once in a while – mainly food. The packages are opened before we get to them to check there is not any counterfeit stuff inside, otherwise it is taken away. Even Recruit Munro gets a package from the 'Navy Mums'. Who are a group of mums who send care packages to recruits who don't have family to send them anything. A really nice gesture. Later in the training one of the Caribbean recruits receives a coat from the Navy

Mums, as they didn't bring one with them to 'go ashore' with. They came in the summer and must have forgotten that it rains a lot here!

To the right of my bunk is Recruit Park, she's a few years older than me; she's really nice but does flirt quite a bit with the male recruits. There is a 'no touch' rule at Raleigh so relationships are a 'no-no'. The recruits are aged from 16 to 37, so there's quite a range but no one really has the energy or time to follow up any 'sparks' with any other recruits to be honest!

We had our class photo this morning. There are 20 of us. In the photo, five girls and 15 boys. I look at the group and wonder if we will all be here in nine weeks' time. We are then herded into seminar rooms again for a talk on our future branches and careers. You would think these would be interesting, but they're not, the Divisional Instructors (DOs) seem to be able to make most things boring. However, I'm relieved as it's a moment of rest amongst a hectic schedule; I can zone out. The instructors introduced our branches; I'm heading for the submarine service so at last we are starting to find out more information on what it involves, because, bizarrely it is really hard to find out information on what you'll actually be doing, but that maybe why it's called the silent service.

Oh, and we had another 'rollicking' from our DOs for leaving our decks in a mess… a daily occurrence pretty much. The DOs have an office on the ground floor of the Nelson Block. Their office door overlooks the entrance, and they can watch us and pick up on things all the time. On the wall by the DO's office is a circular board called

'Remedial Roulette' and it's used for us if they see us doing something wrong. Once I walked out without my beret on and when the DOs saw me, I had to spin the wheel of sin; it landed on 'do ten press-ups' so I had to drop down there and then and give them ten. You'll see recruits doing a forfeit from the Remedial Wheel all the time.

Wednesday 11th September

One thing you learn early on in Raleigh is if someone in the division screws up you are all punished. The IMF staff are brutal when someone makes a mistake in fitness. I actually started to shake from physical exhaustion as some of the circuits they put you through are brutal.

There's an activity you do called 'four corners'; you stand and turn to each corner of the room and do some kind of circuit. We all have to turn at the same time or we receive extra press-ups... turn to the right back corner... ten burpess... it's relentless. You can smile to yourself but cannot be caught outwardly smiling, or you get shouted at. One of the female PT instructors is legendary as she doesn't wear a bra; the recruits call her 'PT Nips' and whenever you see her, she is always 'at attention' and has massive breasts, so you can have a laugh, but only on the inside. If I could have practised more of anything before Raleigh it would have been more burpees, and double time on the spot, although I'm not sure anything could really prepare you for all this.

IMF is followed by more drill work. On Friday, we will have our foot drill exam so need to get this right. There is a lot of screaming and laughing (we don't let the drill instructor see us laugh as that would not be good). Twice a week we do drill. Our drill instructor has a bit of a sense of humour, which is refreshing, especially when some recruits don't seem to know their lefts from their rights.

Friday 13ᵗʰ September

05.30 – The day started at some ungodly hour, and I'm still aching from the 'beasting' the IMF staff gave us on Wednesday. Christ, I am so in need of a sleep in and by a 'sleep in' getting up at seven would be a nice sleep in. It was our foot drill today. We were inspected by a Lieutenant Commander who seemed impressed by our drill. I have to say even though we are a funny old bunch of recruits we're pretty good at drill work. Apparently, my boots were nicely bulled, which is good, as I have spent hours cleaning the buggers. Although an outsider may think sitting in a corridor bullying boots until the late hours would be horrendous there's actually something quite therapeutic about it, it's almost like a routine that takes no thought so you can chat with other recruits and blank out all the other crap you have to deal with. Luckily Port Class passed.

The afternoon was like a Duke of Edinburgh session at school, as it was an introduction to the map and compass, using grid referencing and all that malarkey. I did my bronze Duke of Edinburgh but have forgotten most of it over the last few years, fortunately, it came back to me a bit, but some recruits struggled a bit with the contour lines and the whole grid reading.

We have the odd exam here and there, so today we did a general exam testing our basic knowledge of the Navy that we've been taught in the last few weeks... this is where I find out how much I zoned out in seminars! I hated exams at schools and this is no different, except it is easier as the staff don't notice if you all copy from each other. We all passed our Navy knowledge exams – phew!

22.30 – pipe down and pass out (literally!).

Saturday 14th September

Yay – ok, not quite like a usual weekend. The morning started with an IMF practice session – yippee more rope climbing. Christ, I'm a bit naff at this. My goal is to get further up the rope every time. I feel fitter so, cross fingers, it happens.

The rest of the day involves kit washing, cleaning and phoning my mum. The ironing room is a large room in the basement with rows of ironing boards in. I brought my own iron and luckily my mum paid for a better one, as I read it's worth it, and it is. You spend many hours a day ironing so having good quality iron is key, these are words I never thought would come out of my mouth... ever.

Sunday 15th September

Sunday is the best day. I never thought I could like chapel so much, firstly, Sunday means a sleep in – 7 am and off to chapel for a singsong and tea and biscuits. Honestly, I know it doesn't sound like much but it's everything and gets me though the week knowing I can sit for an hour on a Sunday, sing and have a cuppa afterwards. Those who smoke go and have a quick smoke after chapel before going back to work on kit.

Week 2 Statistics:

Drill training sessions – 2

IMFs – 5

Kit inspections – 2

PVRs – 0

Week 3

Weapon week

Monday 17ᵗʰ September

Week 3 is weapon week. It was the usual early start at 05.30, which interesting I am starting to get used to, followed by scran at 06.20 and a quick march over to the armoury at 07.40.

You have to march everywhere at Raleigh. If you have to walk between buildings; you're not allowed, you can only march. When you look out of your building you'll see random recruits walking around on their own, but they aren't walking they'll be marching. It seems a tad weird to begin with but another anomaly to get used to. Once in a while you're hear an officer shouting at someone because they have been caught walking between buildings; you never know who is watching you.

At the armoury I am given a cleaning kit for the rifle and a helmet. The helmet is heavy and drops a bit on my face even though I have the strap tightened. I wear glasses some of the time but it does not work well with the helmets and rifle sights. I am handed a SA80 rifle and shown how to strip it, clean it and then we spend all day practicing it. Later in the week, we have a weapons test where we have to do these drills on our own. It's not difficult, as such, you just have to remember how to strip it in the right order.

Tuesday 18th September

This was a day of getting to know our rifle even more and practising safety procedures; this involved taking it apart one section at a time, cleaning it and then putting it back together. We had to practise stripping the rifle again and again in preparation for the test on Thursday.

I look forward to the scran at dinnertime. Scran is a time you can sit down and relax. There's always quite a bit of discussion about the quality of the food we get. I am a vegetarian so fare better than most. The vegetarian food was ok, whereas many of the other recruits complained about the meat, as it was unidentifiable.

Scran is the only time you'll see the recruits become a bit wild. Everyone marches to the dining hall in their class: port or starboard, and once you halt outside the dining room, and are dismissed, suddenly there is a complete 'bun fight' with recruits practically clambering over each other to get scran! It's not that there's not enough food, there's plenty, but everyone is soooo hungry, everyone is starving and can't wait to get some food down them. It's actually similar to the dinner queue at school, with recruits trying to push in and other recruits practically fighting for position. The class leaders are in charge of the classes, so there's no instructors there to tell us off. It's actually quite funny, as it doesn't matter how old or mature you are, when you're starving it all 'goes out the window'. You have 30 minutes to march to the dining hall and eat, that's it, and if you're running late for any reason you have less than 30 minutes, so eating scran has to be really quick. It feels so good to have hot food in you or any food actually. At Raleigh you can't snack between meals so in the first few weeks you're limited to meal times.

Wednesday 19th September

Today we did Dismounted Close Contact Training (DCCT) which is like lasar tag, which a number of the male recruits got very excited by. I think to some of them it is like one of their PlayStation Games and they get just as excited. Sometimes I do worry some of them just 'join up' as an extension of some kind of fictional belief that the military is like a computer war game.

Thursday 20th September

At last, I get to shoot on the range but only after passing the weapon-handling test. Recruits get two chances to pass and if they fail they are 'put back' a week. I failed the first attempt just through nerves; it is stressful. The instructors call you into a room and you have to strip your rifle, clean it and then reassemble it. You get another attempt after more practice and most do pass, including myself, thank heavens. Unfortunately, a couple of recruits don't pass and they are 'back classed' to the division behind us. Recruit Miller who had been 'back classed', as he failed but passed this time, joined our division today; he passed.

The recruits in your class change a bit over the ten weeks; some of the recruits are 'back classed' for failing something, or they get injured, and you have a few new faces from an older division, who themselves were back classed and are now fit/good enough to continue. If you are 'back classed' you have to go to Crean, a division of its own. Even if you are at Crean you still follow a similar routine to the other divisions. You still have to wake up at 05.30 and have deck checks and kit checks. The only difference being if the recruit is in Crean for an injury, they have rehab work on their injury during the day and have to help with tasks around the base.

Friday 21st September

Today was 'wet and dry' day at MTU, as it is known at Raleigh. Quite haunting to march pass the older Raleigh buildings on the fringe of the base. We passed armed guards and Marines working out until we eventually got to the range. You march there with your rifle and it feels like you are 'off to war'. This is a day controlled by the Marines... lovely. They showed 'us' survival techniques and how to use our rations. I was issued with a 'bivvy' and shown what to do with it. Rations are not as bad as recruits make out. It's mostly dried food that you rehydrate with hot water, and the hot chocolate is a pretty good brew to be honest.

This activity is called 'wet and dry' as towards the end of the day, fully clothed, I was hosed down with a hose pipe and soaked. Once wet I got very cold very quickly. If you were on watch during the night you had to keep your wet kit on...it was bloody freezing. There were six of us on duty shivering our way through the two-hour duty. The only positive is you get to know your fellow recruits a bit more and some have some varied backgrounds. Everyone is very serious about the Royal Navy, some of the boys have waited all their life to join, but I wasn't like that it almost felt like this was something I had to do after not wanting to continue with my A-levels. I almost fell into it, because my mum wanted me to do something worthwhile with my life, but you meet some recruits who have dreamt about this moment. I definitely did not dream about being sprayed with cold water and having to do a night duty in the freezing cold. You seem to get one sadistic recruit that seems to enjoy the misery though!

Saturday 22nd September

We woke up early on Saturday and went back to the Nelson Block. Luckily, we had all weekend to 'turn around' out kits, as they were soaked and muddy. Trying to get them dry is no mean feat as there are no dryers just a dryer room that smells of wet trainers. By the end of the day I was starting to get more stressed, as nothing seems to be drying and having wet kit is a kit inspection failure.

Although Sundays are more restful, I do get a bit homesick on the weekend, I think it's because I have some time to actually think I miss home. There is no time to think during the week so it is not an issue. Raleigh is a bit of a rollercoaster of emotions. My mum says it's nearly as bad for her listening to me recount what I am going through, and all the stressed phone calls, but it can't be as bad as being here. Another exhausting week over with.

Week 3 Statistics:

Drill training sessions – 4

IMFs – 6

Kit inspections – 4

PVRs – 0

Week 4

Piers Cellers

Monday 23rd September

The new week started with a kit muster; our first proper kit muster whilst at Raleigh. I spent the whole of the weekend preparing for it. All my kit was properly laid out on my bed, named, shirts ironed into A4 size in the exact specification asked of us, and luckily, I passed, but we didn't all pass. Some had a warning but the 'team' spirit is kicking in, and recruits are realising we all need to help each other. Some recruits are better at some areas than others are, so there's always someone to advise. It's slightly soul destroying when you fail because you missed one small aspect of the kit. There are three tier warnings and then you can be 'back classed' or 'out'. Tier 3 is the first warning and at this point the recruit is told by their DO what the warning is for and what they need to do to reach the required standard. The Tier 2 warning comes from a more senior officer. A Tier 1 warning is the most serious and comes from the Officer in Command. If you don't meet the standard required for the Tier 1 then you will be Discharged Unsuitable During Training (DUDT). Most people say it's three strikes then out, which is true, but I found it was more to do with what the warning was for and the severity of the mistake. A lot seemed to receive warnings for kit, but I believe if you receive a warning for attitude/ disobeying orders it's taken more seriously. Also, if you give 100% all the time, and are respectful, your DO will be more supportive if you receive a tier warning.

Tuesday 24th September

This morning we had IMF followed directly by drill and division inspections, because of this we had to go to IMF in parade rig. When we arrive at the Physical Education Hall the IMF instructor stood at the front on a wooden block, looking down at us, so there was no escape from his gaze. If you did something wrong they'd notice which is more pain for all. Unfortunately, when I got to IMF today I realised I had forgotten my white socks so the physical education instructors made me run all the way back to the Nelson Block to get them. When I got back the instructors made me do push-ups, in my parade boots, so the freshly bullied boots didn't look like they were bullied anymore and had scratches all over them. Trying to do IMF in boots is hard. I think IMF gets more brutal as the weeks go by. A couple of recruits were late and got a right 'rollicking'. And as always we all suffered and had to do 20 burpees.

We had our scran at lunch then went off to Piers Cellars for exercise Daring Leap. Piers Cellars is an old quarry full of water by the Cornish coast. It's great to get off base, as you start to feel claustrophobic not being allowed out of the compound. Exercise Daring Leap is quite a laugh, as you have to rope up pullies across a section of water and get a 'casualty', who is in fact your Divisional Instructor, across the water using a pulley system. There is the usual race between Port and Starboard classes. When we got there though, the water was only a foot tall, and there wasn't much water at all, so the DIs opened the floodgates and tons of cold sea water came flooding in. The water was bloody freezing and we only had our greens on. At times it was quite a laugh as we raced across the water inlet but when we stopped we got cold quickly. When you are cold and wet a cup of tea is everything... little things really count here.

That evening we had the campfires going, and were 'spinning dits' with the DOs, we ate a well-earned meal. For the first time the DOs were quite friendly. After dinner we had to make up different plays illustrating the Naval Service Core Values of Commitment, Courage, Discipline, Respect for Others, Integrity and Loyalty. I have to say some of the plays were a bit 'naff', and unprepared, and felt like they were being made up as the recruits went along, but our group wasn't quite up to *Macbeth* standard either.

We slept in bunk beds that night but were pretty chilly in our building. We had to do duties overnight, in groups of six. I was on duty 3 – 5 am, which meant standing by a fence in the freezing cold trying to stay awake until the early hours of the morning.

Wednesday 25th September
Around 4 am the fire alarm was set off by the DOs, on purpose, to get us up for early morning IMF. The PT instructor comes with. Joy! The PT instructor gets to put us through the IMF even though you're away from

Raleigh. The IMF is followed by a brisk ten km walk, with map and compass, which may not seem too bad but with a heavy Bergen on, and the rain pouring down, it soon became a strain. The way to get through it is head down and 'zone out' and ignore any blisters that start to throb. It was a point-to-point exercise so we walked to different points on the map, within a time period.

In the afternoon we did the assault course, timed, just in case we had any energy left! I didn't mind the assault course, but I got a little scared walking along the wall and jumping off at the end. The wall is a good seven feet up, which seems a lot higher once you're on it. You start by doing a team warm up with the PT instructors and then lay on the ground in a sit-up position at the start of the course before you go. The whole course is timed. It consists of climbing with ropes, running along the tops of walls, jumping between the walls and metal bars, rolling under wires, jumping over wires, crawling along gravel, running through water, climbing over large tunnels, crawling through large waterlogged tunnels, and just when you think you can't do anymore you have to run up a hill at the end. The best time is around 12 minutes, which may not sound like long, but feels much longer. You are constantly being shouted at either by the instructors or your fellow class mates. It ends with you all dropping into the assault course pond so the DIs can take photos of you to put on social media.

Thursday 26th September
Thursday started with a recovery swim and run. We then had to prepare for another kit muster tomorrow which

was a nightmare due to most of the kit being soaking wet! The only good thing about today was we were fitted for our Number 1 uniform for the passing out ceremony, and although this was exciting, I was so tired it was hard to be excited. The Number 1 uniform is the posh uniform we wear for our passing out parade and they do look very smart.

Friday September 27th

This is the end of a very long week but today we still had another IMF session before watching our seniors pass out. It's very heartening to see the senior class of Nelson pass out, as you get to know the class well, and they do try and help you when you first get to Raleigh. I made a quick phone call to my mum tonight as I was so exhausted I needed some kind, encouraging words. I was really suffering and thinking about PVR-ing, but after a chat with the 'Bish' (Chaplain), and my Mum, I felt more encouraged. The Bish, as he's known around base, is very easy to talk to and encouraging; he acts as the base counsellor when recruits need a chat about their worries. It doesn't matter if you're not a devout Christian, or are of another faith, he's open to anyone who needs to talk.

Saturday 28th September

We were supposed to end this week with a visit to the China Fleet Club. China Fleet Country Club is set in 180 acres of countryside located on the Tamar estuary, and recruits get to go there to lounge in their pool and hot tubs, eat nice food and relax before heading back to Raleigh; it's a real treat that all recruits look forward to.

However, the Friday kit muster went really bad so the DOs were having doubts, and unfortunately due to the behaviour of the boys in Nelson Division it was a definite 'no'. Over the weekend, the officer came in to keep an eye on the division classes. You would think by the time boys (men) get to their late teens and early 20s they would have matured a bit, well think again! I swear sticking 30 boys/men in a room together brings the worst out of them... it's like they're back at school.

Last night at about 10 pm, just before lights out, we were all get called outside, onto the divisional square, by the weekend staff. The boys in Nelson were caught having a flip flop fight by the weekend officer. The flip flop fight got out of control and the boys started hitting each other with the hoover and socks filled with notebooks. The DO caught them, so we all were called out to the divisional square in the pouring rain. The officer gave us all an absolute 'rollocking'. He was shouting at us so loudly the recruits from the other blocks started hanging out the windows and laughing. The DO was not impressed. He turned to the recruits and told them all to turn off their lights off and 'f**k off', suddenly all the other block's lights went off, however we could tell they were still all at their windows watching. We had to stand out in the pouring rain until the DO allowed us to go back in. Once the DO left us in the square at attention, the recruits from the other blocks started singing Oasis: 'Nelson can't wait.... '. When the DO came back out he made the main culprits do burpees whilst chanting 'I won't do flip flop fights again'. Boys seem to become a bit primal when you put them all together.

Week 4 Statistics:

Drill training sessions – 6

IMFs – 6

Kit inspections – 4

PVRs – 0

Week 5

Seamanship Training

Monday 30th September

Yes, I have made it to week five... a miracle but nonetheless I am here. Strange I thought as soon as I hit week five I would leave, but I probably won't at the moment. There's only six weeks to go so I may as well try and make it to the end. We started the week by completing another timed 2.4 km RNFT run. I was nearly a minute quicker than four weeks ago. I'm definitely thinner and fitter than when I joined, and although I am tired, I feel good.

The high ropes and the 'leap of faith' followed the run which is a test of courage and overcoming your fears. The ropes don't seem too high until you climb them and look down. We had to climb a very tall post, which is about 40 feet tall and then once you get to the top you jump off. Even though the recruits have safety ropes on, it does feel very scary jumping off into thin air that high up, but you just have to not think about it and just do it. Luckily, when I was younger I went on a number of summer camps and they had similar rope challenges on their courses, but some recruits absolutely 'pooped' themselves. There was a lot of encouragement from fellow recruits and also a lot of swearing... 'Sweet mother of .... f**king hell'... when a recruit got to the top of the post the other recruits cheered them on and encouraged them, if the recruit didn't jump they got a warning. You need to show commitment so you have to 'dig deep'.

Tuesday 1ˢᵗ October

We spent the next few days with seamanship training, which was a relief because it involved sitting, something I haven't done anything of so far at Raleigh. You literally never sit down apart from when you go to bed, and chapel on a Sunday. We did a lot of winching and knot tying. There is a long piece of rope, we all line up against, that we practise tying our knots on. It can be a bit boring but I'm happy to be bored at this stage.

In the afternoon, we took part in a simulation of a RAS rig. The RAS is replenishment at sea, when a ship transfers food/water/fuel and even personnel to another ship without having to go alongside. Raleigh has one of the world's leading replenishment-at-sea (RAS) trainer, apparently, which means we can practice RAS. The RAS rig is made up of two concrete platforms that simulate the decks of ships and we practiced moving fuel lines between the two. The trainer allows the transfer of 25 five-tonnes, every hour, across a 55-metre gap that separates the two platforms.

Friday 4ᵗʰ October

Today we had some seminars on the Law of Armed Conflict, and for the first time we were part of the Divisions for the passing out parade. We have obviously made the standard as we can now be seen marching in public. Later that day we had an IMF full of sprints and on the spot marching. What's funny is there's always someone who gets more warnings and is always late, sometimes the recruit is just unorganised or just 'isn't with it'. Recruit MacDonald was like that. He's a nice chap but is always being caught doing something wrong, nothing substantial, but nothing ever is here it may just be a speck of dirt on your shoe, late for gym, bit of fluff on your belt. All minor warnings, but they all add up, and before you know it you have a Tier 1 warning. They say at Raleigh being able to follow instructions is the most important part; the Navy can't have sailors not following orders on a ship or in a submarine.

Saturday 5th October

Interestingly, a lot of recruits are like me they have no Plan B. It's the Navy, McDonald's, or the supermarket and no one wants to end up back stocking shelves. This is one thing I keep in my mind that this is the best option and the alternative career choices are not great, so when things get tough I remember the alternatives. There are some recruits who are serious about 'PVR-ing'. Some recruits have made it through the first four weeks but have decided it just isn't for them, and it's easy to see why, but I figure the first four weeks are the worst so I might as well keep going.

The morning started with deck games and a football match between Port and Starboard classes. I'm not footballer, but it was a lot of laughs and you have to laugh when you can.

Sunday 6th October

Chapel – ahh relax.

Week 5 Statistics:

IMFs – 6

PVR – 4

Week 6

Jupiter Point

Monday 7th October

The week started with physical training. A bit of a brutal start to the week with a 'beasting' from the PT staff. We were outside, for this session, and had to carry one of our colleagues on our backs around obstacles and up and down mounds. There is an outside area where we also complete fitness tasks that involve moving tractor tyres around a court, metals bars for pull-ups and hammers to bash the tyres with. It's pretty tiring and some recruits really struggle but as a team we pull together to get through it.

Tuesday 8th October

07.45- We went off to Jupiter Point this morning, which apparently was something to look forward to and should be fun. Jupiter Point is the jetty down by the river. It has a very pretty backdrop and it's a great relief to see some countryside. We started with a 'swimmer of the watch' brief which involved jumping of the side of the ship with a wetsuit, swimming to a casualty and bringing them back to the ship. The casualty then was placed on a stretcher and hoisted up onto the ship with the ship hoist.

In the afternoon we were split into different teams and assigned a boat. We learnt sea navigation, man overboard drills and going alongside a pontoon. Tonight we spent the night on an old minesweeper called the *Brecon* which was extra fun as it is Halloween and doing night duties on an old minesweeper is fairly spooky. HMS *Brecon* is a Hunt-class mine countermeasures vessel that served in the Falklands conflict and is now the training ship for HMS Raleigh. The ship is moored out from Jupiter Point and is about 200 feet long on the River Lynher. It's smallish but still fun to be off base.

Wednesday 9th October

After an early breakfast on the *Brecon* we were transferred to the 'RIBS' which is a massive adrenaline fix for the morning. We practised going alongside and man overboard at Jupiter Point. The weather was sunny so it felt a bit like a holiday! This was followed by more navigation exercises but the sun was out and the countryside was looking stunning so not a bad day at all.

Thursday 10th October

Back to earth this morning with IMF 8; more sprints, circuit training and ropes. We did 'camp circuits' which consist of running around a circuit as quickly as you can with points where we did different exercises.

Friday 11th October

Everyone talks about the stretcher run... it's notorious! And today is the day. All the class was really nervous. The stretcher run consists of a three mile circuit with 'extras', none other than a 80 kg dummy called 'Fred'. The run is brutal and all about teamwork. It involves crawls, dragging each other, sprints, bunny hopping, going up and down a hill, and this carries on for about two hours. We have to give maximum effort at all time, and work as a team, which not everyone does. You can feel it when someone isn't pulling their weight as the stretcher starts to droop on one corner. It's absolutely shattering and at the end I just fell on the floor and don't move. Not everyone can do it, Recruit Barrow just sat down halfway through and said she couldn't move anymore; she just gave up. By the end five recruits end up injured and in Med Bay, and a couple of the recruits just sit on the grass crying.

Saturday and Sunday 12th and 13th October

In the morning, we practised our weapon drill followed by time in the gym rope climbing. There is a technique to rope climbing, but it doesn't work for me and my palms really sting. After gym we all spend the rest of the weekend preparing kit.

This weekend was a bit depressing, as one of my friends from school phoned me as she was feeling suicidal. It's really hard as my life is moving rapidly and hers is not. She suffers from depression and is quite miserable. I have known her since I was born, so I do care, but it's difficult to support her when I, myself, am facing so much. I would never have said this a few weeks ago, but I do believe all young people would benefit from a stint in the Royal Navy or services. The training teaches you that you can survive without your phone and social media. You are so busy you don't even have time to feel sorry for yourself.

Week 6 Statistics:

IMFs – 8

Kit inspections – 5

PVRs – 4

Week 7

Exercise Hidden Dragon

Monday 14th October

Another important kit muster this morning. It's the same drill as all the others: wash and iron all your kit, check your name tags and de-fluff everything. The kit musters become tougher as the weeks progress, and you spend

ages de-threading your kit. Ugh – I failed the kit muster, I can't believe it, after spending hours on my kit I fail because there's a bit of fluff on my Velcro. It is so nuts, but you have to 'play the game'. I'm at Week 7 so the end is in sight, failing isn't an option. I am called to 'the table' to receive a warning, but really want to get this right.

Kit locker

A new bunch of girls joined our division today, Nelson juniors. Being a junior comes with both its advantages and disadvantages. The advantage is you have seniors (that's me) who you can ask for help and advice, just as I did in Week 1, but the disadvantage is as a junior you have to go through some 'activities' such as seagull counting and cleaning the pipes with Brasso.

In the afternoon we had a talk on the history of the Royal Navy concluded with an interactive computer game on Nelson's war strategy followed by branch talks on the submarine service.

Tuesday 15th October

It was our 'passing out' practice today followed by more map and compass exercise for our weekend on Dartmoor. This was our final full practice before our Guard Selection on Wednesday. We went through all the drill marches we had been taught over and over again to perfection. This was an especially amusing drill practice as Recruit Jones wasn't feeling well at all and had stomach ache. He rose his hand to ask to be excused, by the drill instructor, as he needed 'the head' but the drill instructor was having none of it and kept telling him to 'stop dancing around'. Eventually Jones bent over, let out an enormous fart and the rest followed. Not pleasant at all. At this point the drill instructor dismissed him to go and get changed. Poor boy he nearly passed out, apparently it was a dodgy sausage at breakfast that caused it.

Wednesday 16th October

We had guard selection this morning which was a competition between Port and Starboard on who does the best drill, Port side won! Yes, that's my team! After completing our drill in front of the commander we went to the drill shed, our win was announced, and the class leaders received a small trophy of a guard. We are definitely on schedule to win the 'Ganges'. We spend at least an hour practising our drill on the parade ground with music to keep us in time. We do it again and again before we go head-to-head with Starboard class. You want to prove you're better than the other team and be your best. You feel some pride in what you are doing, which I never would have guessed I would have felt seven weeks ago.

Afterwards we left for Dartmoor and Exercise Hidden Dragon. Tonight we all camped in tents. Not the wonderful modern 'pop up' tents no, no, they were the old canvas tents you use on D of E expeditions. There were three of us in a tent, and I shared mine with Recruit Haddock and Park. Although it was cold out, three people in a small tent kept us warm. The best part was the heads block, as they were new and warm. The DOs timed us in the toilet so we didn't hang out inside for too long; you literally had a few minutes to do your stuff and get out otherwise they came and got you out. Apparently, they now check us as a previous group were found in the toilets, with their sleeping bags camping out, to avoid the cold of the tents; there were 30 recruits squeezed into six cubicles! To be fair the toilets were very warm. I'm not completely sure a toilet floor is better than a tent, but I suppose it depends on how cold and wet it is outside.

Friday 18th October

This morning the DOs made us wash in a local lake before our hike. The lads had to shave in the freezing cold so there was a lot of swearing going on unless the Chief was around. Using our navigation skills we did a team trek across Dartmoor, with our Bergens on, going from 'point-to-point'. It was gruelling and the weather wasn't on our side, at all, in fact it just poured down. What was really neat is the marines were out practicing some kind of manoeuvre and there were helicopters flying overhead, so it was quite exciting and felt like a scene from *Apocalypse Now*. With low-flying helicopters and Marines running around firing blanks it felt like we were in a war zone. As we hiked from 'point-to-point' we found the terrain was quite challenging. I had hiked quite a bit before: Lake District, Brecon Beacons, Snowdonia, but Dartmoor has its own uniqueness. The ground is wet and feels like you are continually walking on damp moss which is quite heavy going on tired legs. The grass is knee height in places and it is easy to get lost. We were so lost at one point that my mate, who was reading the map, wasn't concentrating on where he was walking and fell face first into a massive mud ditch; it took us a good ten minutes to get him out. There is an old prison on Dartmoor where French Napoleonic French prisoners of war were sent. Some of the prisoners escaped to Dartmoor, apparently, and were never found again, well that's what the DOs told us, and you can see why as there's not many landmarks to go by, and if the weather was bad, it would be near impossible to navigate the terrain.

The teams were made up of about ten recruits and in the evening we camped out together and ate our ration packs. Team spirit was high, and there was a sense of relief, but Recruit Singh hurt her ankle during her march and was 'back classed' to Crean, until her ankle got better. Singh was in tears with pain and disappointment. It's a shame as it means she won't pass out with us in two weeks. She wasn't the only recruit in Crean from the Dartmoor trek, as there were a few hurt legs and ankles that meant the recruit had to be 'back classed' whilst their injury passed. The girls and boys who had a small physique really suffered on this exercise because the Bergens are heavy. The next morning we packed away ready for the coach ride back to Raleigh, via the pub for lunch. The stop at the pub was a nice touch that cheered everyone up no end. I am still under 18 so couldn't partake in the beer (not that you were allowed) but having a Coke was bliss. I had a big plate of cheesy chips whereas some of the lads had massive plates of steak and chips, and I think because of all the physical exertion of the day, they then threw up the £30 meals into the toilet.

Sunday 20th October

This morning church was followed by shore leave, which meant it was the first time we were allowed to leave the base on our own. Unfortunately, the weather was horrendous and the Torpoint ferry was out of action, so the only alternative was to take a taxi ride all the way around to Plymouth. A few recruits took the taxi, just to escape the compound of HMS Raleigh, but I and a few others decided not to bother and worked on our kit; it still meant an afternoon of leisure though.

Week 7 Statistics:

IMFs – 10

Kit inspections – 5

PVR – 6

Week 8

Havoc

Monday 21st October

05.30 – call of hands

It's Week 8 and it's starting to feel like 'passing out' might be a reality. After scran we packed up to start our first aid course which was quite an enjoyable experience. We learnt about DRSABC – Danger, response, shout, airways, breathing and circulation. Followed by dressing wounds and CAT – combat, application and tourniquet. After lunch, we did putting our mates into the recovery position and then practised different medical situations. Oh, and I also spent two hours polishing my boots after dinner... bliss.

Tuesday 22nd October

After lunch we marched to the fire school for Havoc, the sinking ship simulator. We entered the engine room which is at the bottom of the ship covered in holes. You start at the top of the compartment, as it has two floors, and when it starts to flood you go down the stairs. We were told that a missile was inbound and would strike the ship, and we had to brace as it struck the hull. It is surprising how real it feels; I started to feel quite scared as the warning sounds started to go off. Suddenly all the lights went out and tons of water started to fill the engine room. Our task was to try and block up the holes with the bags of wooden wedges that we had been given. I'm stood hammering wood wedges into the holes, wood expands so it actually works really well. As all this was going on Havoc starts to move side to side. By this time the water was up to our hips and we were all trying hard to control the flow of water. It was a lot harder and a lot more realistic than we first expected, also the water was extremely cold. After 25 minutes the water stopped and the lights came back on.

The morning was fun in some ways and scary in others; a fire on a ship or submarine is very dangerous and literally needs to be extinguished in minutes. We spent the rest of the day learning how to put out fires in different scenarios. A really fun afternoon as we got to wear fire service gear with fire jackets and helmets.

Wednesday 23rd October

Today we did our GSR (general service respirator) check which is known as the 'gassing'. I had heard quite a lot of stories/rumours about the gas training and it sounded quite scary. You never know if the stories are true or just there to scare the new recruits. We marched down to the gas chamber and were given the gas masks to put on. The masks are large and cover your whole face with two large filters on either side. The most nervous part is waiting to go into the room to do the exercise. You all go into the room in small groups so you get to watch the rest of the class go in first, and come out coughing and spluttering, before it is your turn.

The group before us come out of the gas chamber spitting stuff out their mouths and wheezing before our group is called in. Five of us go into the room and it is explained the CS (tear) gas will be released into the room and we need to breathe through our masks. We are then directed to take off our masks and recite our service number. Whilst watching the others I decide to try and not breathe into the gas when it's my turn. I hold my breath for as long as I can, and then cite my service number before running out the room to breathe the fresh air. It didn't feel as bad as the 'stories' I've heard and to be honest the waiting to go in to 'the room' was worse. My eyes were a bit itchy and sore, but I personally didn't feel scared at any time. I believe the recruits can react differently to the gas, but everyone in my class seemed to be ok.

Thursday 24th October

Nelson Division all had their Level 2 first aid tests this morning, and we all passed. This was swiftly followed by more parade and drill practice. After lunch we had a gym session; it had been a quite a while since the last one so a bit of a shock to the system. We all had to do the famous bleep and the rope test. It was a close run for a few recruits but after a 'rope off' the PT Staff finally decided on the six that would be the PT superiors, it wasn't me, but well done to the ones that were the fastest, as it was brutal.

Friday 25th October

We had more seminars on the RN this morning followed by the assault course. The exercise involved climbing ropes and going through concrete tubes filled with water. The assault course is all about finishing as a team, so you are constantly cheering on your mates and getting them to finish quicker. After we had all finished the DOs made the Port team submerge themselves in a big pool of cold water. This was all followed by a quick shower before changing into our Number 1s and proudly marching across the parade ground to support the class ahead that was passing out.

Saturday and Sunday 26th and 27th October

Today we did more PT followed by revision for our NGT exam. Saturday night we were allowed to go for a drink at the NAAFI. One good thing about HMS Raleigh is it has a coffee house on the base, of course you're not allowed to go there until much later in your training, and you have to earn the privilege, but nonetheless it I know it existed and it was something to look forward to.

Week 8 Statistics:

IMFs – 10

Kit inspections – 6

PVR – 8

Week 9

Bright Diamond

Monday 28th October

After the usual morning scran, and cleaning stations, the class headed off to the Heritage Centre for a series of lectures on various topics that will help us gain more from our naval careers. Today, we had lectures on financial awareness, personal insurance and personal administration in order to prepare us for Phase 2 training and our later careers.

Later we were back on the parade ground being introduced to our 'arms drill at the halt' routine. Arms drill at the halt is a synchronised drill to music, in this case the music was the theme tune to *Rocky*, which we'll be using during our passing out parade in a week's time. I quite liked having the music as it kept me to time and added a bit of fun to the drill practice. After the drill session we had another demanding IMF refresher session with our PTIs. This was the first of consecutive sessions of IMF sessions, we were exhausted, but morale was still high at the end of the day, because the end was in sight.

Tuesday 29th October

We started off with the NGT exam, where we were tested on all the basic naval knowledge that we needed. Even though we had all studied hard and prepared ourselves, we were all still understandably nervous but we didn't need to be, everyone in the class passed. However, after the exam came another IMF session and the best way to describe it was that it was an absolute 'beasting'. This was followed, far too soon, by another drill session, to start properly getting to grips with our crucial passing out routine. We finally finished the day off with a rather entertaining introduction to the action assault course.

Wednesday 30th October

This morning we had a drill session followed the IMF, which was a better session and we were starting to show progress. It was our final IMF, before the IMF pass out (last one), so even though we were exhausted we were all focused on trying our best. After the morning we had a seminar on drugs awareness and the Royal Navy, not surprisingly there are random drugs tests in the Royal Navy, and there is a no tolerance attitude to taking drugs; if you are caught you're out, it as simple as that.

We still have one more 'off Raleigh' exercise to do before 'passing out' and that's exercise Bright Diamond. In the afternoon we packed our bags and boarded a coach for Jupiter Point.

Upon arriving at Jupiter Point we were moved to the docks by everyone's favourite improvised ferry; the gangway needs a lot of work! The IMF sessions have prepared us well for the rope work needed on the aging gangway.

For the next couple of days HMS *Brecon* would be our home. As mentioned, the *Brecon* is a retired minehunter, stuck to a concrete bed just off Jupiter Point. We were shown around the ship, received an introductory brief, prepared our beds and set up our watch routine. Each class has a night where they need to keep watches. We were also given an assignment: each class had to prepare a presentation on one of the arms of the Royal Navy. Luckily, we had been given our topics days earlier, so we had ample time to gather the information. The best part was playing a game of 'hunt the thimble' on the ship, where I was the thimble; it was great. I got to hide in a ship cupboard for 20 minutes whilst the rest of the Nelson class tried to find me. It is a 'man overboard' drill and it was great fun, especially as I got to sit for 20 minutes!

Thursday 31st October

It was disaster scenario day; a HQ tent was set up, reconnaissance teams were sent out and the medical team was standing by. Over the next couple of hours we were exposed to a range of extreme yet plausible disaster scenarios. The realism of the exercise was enhanced further by rain, in place to better simulate hurricane conditions. I was medical personnel and had to use my first aid training to assess survivors of the hurricane. We tried to take it seriously, even though we had friends who were playing injured people, to be honest they made up the injured people well, with fake injuries. We had to evaluate the injured and decide the course of action. One of the injured people was a colleague of mine that was a few weeks ahead of us. He was in hold over before starting the Phase 2 submarine training. It's funny you meet fellow recruits at Raleigh who then go on to be friends for your career. Robert, who I treated that day for a damaged leg, went through Phase 2 with me. We met again in Faslane, as we were in the same branch together, but different submarines.

Friday 1st November

Today was a rather easy and relaxed day. We started off by watching a documentary on the Royal Navy and their role in disaster relief after the devastating results of Hurricane Earl in the Caribbean. We then headed off to HMS Raleigh. When we arrived at HMS Raleigh we started on our distress exercise, which aside from making a bridge went rather well.

Saturday 2nd November

Today we were giving shore leave with the main objective of buying an outlandish shirt for the passing out dinner. Most of us went to the charity shops in Plymouth, as it's generally a good source of weird shirts. I found a bright Hawaiian shirt with bananas and pineapples on, perfect for a night out.

Sunday 3rd November

Another exciting day to end off an exciting week. Today was the first day we could wear and show off our Number 1 kit to the juniors at church. It was emotional going to our last church in our Phase 1 training period. Everyone belted out all the songs with pride and excitement, they then proceeded to take a ridiculous number of photos together after the service. One thing you come to realise though is the Number 1 uniform is a bit itchy. I think it's wool and after a bit is feels very warm and a bit scratchy. It does look good and when you first wear the uniform, you wear it with a sense of pride but after a while you dread having to put it on, as it takes a while and feels very warm. Luckily, you don't wear it very often. In Phase 2 it became a punishment to make a recruit go put on their Number 1s!

Week 9 Statistics:

IMFs – 12

Kit inspections – 7

PVRs – 10

Week 10

Passing out

Monday 4th November

This is the last week, however it is still a tough one, but knowing it is all over in five days helps. We are all so close to the end but you can still mess up in the last week. Spirits are high and the girls are singing whilst cleaning their boots, but as they say 'it's not over until the fat lady sings'. It's a busy week before the passing out parade and we still have our last IMF session, assault course competitions and last drill session to go.

Today we have our last IMF test. Everyone is really nervous, as it all comes down to this. It starts with the 2.4 km run then off to the sports hall for a 'beasting'. We start by doing press ups, burpees, climbing ropes, sprints and push our bodies to their limit. It's knackering and we all have to pass, it is not an individual pass; we all pass or no one passes. We all passed. Thank god for that.

Tuesday 5th November

The Commander of the base did the rounds this morning. We know he's arrived as he's 'piped in' as he enters the mess. He's met by the door by our class leader and then carries on inspecting the mess and us. He asks me what I found hardest about the ten weeks. In reality it's just really relentless, and tiring, with no let up. Yes, I miss my family and yes the IMF and phys ed is a bit brutal at times, but it's all doable. The worst part is it is nonstop with no rest. You don't get a day off, you don't get an afternoon off – it's just nonstop from morning to night, but everyone is going through it, and everyone is exhausted, you just have to get your head down and 'soldier on'. We learn to talk to each other, whinge and moan to each other… having a good moan helps. I complained to my mum a lot on the phone; it was my out pouring every week and she listened and told me that there was only 10, 9, 8, 7… weeks to go and once you've passed the halfway mark there's no point PVRing because you're on the home straight.

Wednesday 6th November

We have to run the Raleigh Assault Course, this morning, with Port and Starboard competing against each other in their final battle. Port class take today's win as well as the Ganges Trophy, which help our morale no end.

It's a fun night tonight as we went for our passing out dinner with our Division Officers. We all wore our outlandish shirts and head off for a nice meal in Plymouth, followed by a lot of drinking to celebrate. It was a great laugh and a nice way to end off basic training, especially as you can watch your divisional staff get drunk. Our Royal Marine drill instructor had a few too many and ended up on the table dancing to music; it was hilarious; we had to practically carry him home.

Friday 8ᵗʰ November

No more kit cleaning, drill, IMF. I swear I spend four hours a day cleaning kit, no more as today is passing out day. This is the day that makes it all worth it. We have to be packed up, cleaned and in our Number 1s ready for passing out. Everyone shows a mix of jubilation and fear as we have to parade in front of all our friends and family. I haven't seen my mum for 10 weeks and cannot wait to see them and see their faces as I march out in my Number 1s! It's November so chilly but luckily, it's sunny today.

We start by going to the theatre to collect our epaulets, and it was the first time I saw my family in the auditorium; they were in the front row, so I couldn't miss them! I felt very embarrassed and was very nervous. We weren't allowed to talk to them but they were waving, which made me happy. What is nice is if any of the overseas recruits don't have family, at passing out, the families that are present are told who these recruits are in advance, so they clap and cheer for them. There's something so warm and supportive about it all and the DOs show that they are human! After receiving our epaulets, we run for scran before we have to change into our Number 1s for our Passing Out parade and Ceremonial Divisions.

After getting changed we step out onto the parade ground for the last time. Everyone looked so smart and the HM Royal Marine band is playing uplifting music, such as 'Heart of Oak' and 'Nancy Lee'. Our inspecting officer for passing out is the Captain from the Britannia RN College (where the officers train). We are the East and the Lead Guard, which means we are first out of the 'hangers' and lead out on to the parade ground. We stand on the parade ground, before the inspection, and the Captain walks around inspecting are uniform and making general 'chit chat'. It's really nerve racking but the subsequent arms drill goes well, and I particularly like the ripple drill, but you're too nervous to really enjoy it. We give the final salute to the inspecting officer and then form up for the 'Step routine' as we all march up the steps either side of the VIPs until we halt and then throw our hats in the air. I never thought I would make it to this point but I am filled with pride, sadness and relief all at the same time. Some of our friends who are in Crean with injuries, came to watch us pass out so there were many hugs and goodbyes, and of course, we then joined our families after not seeing them for ten weeks.

After HMS Raleigh we all went our separate ways to our Phase 2 training. I, and a few others, stay at Raleigh for our Phase 2. Submarine training is at Raleigh, but many of my teammates go off to Winchester, to the catering school, and the engineers go to Collingwood. By the time I finished my Phase 2 submariner training some of my Raleigh friends are already on the surface fleet ships. Two years on from basic training I can look at my Snapchat and find my fellow Raleigh teammates scattered all around the world, in different vessels and across all the branches.

Passing Out Parade

What I learnt about Raleigh:

- Do what you are told and don't question it no matter how much you might disagree with it.

- Help each other; if you help your mates, they will help you.

- Try your best. Give 100% all the time, even if you fail at something. If you are giving maximum effort your DOs are more likely to be supportive. Try not to piss your DOs off, although you do not realise it, they are trying to help you and get you through the ten weeks.

- You want to push yourself that is what it's all about, you need to show improvement in everything by the end of the ten weeks.

- No matter how bad you think it is, it will be worth it in the end.

- A career in the Royal Navy is not like the Basic Training at Raleigh. Basic Training is what you have to go through; I see it as a gateway and in this case a gateway to Phase 2 training and the rest of your Navy career.

End of Basic Training

Printed in Great Britain
by Amazon

18370231R00045